THE LEATHERWOOD GOD

The Leatherwood God

(1869-70)

A Source of William Dean Howells's

Novel of the Same Name

IN TWO VERSIONS

BY

Richard H. Taneyhill

FACSIMILE REPRODUCTIONS

WITH AN INTRODUCTION

BY

George Kummer

GAINESVILLE, FLORIDA

SCHOLARS' FACSIMILES & REPRINTS

1966

SCHOLARS' FACSIMILES & REPRINTS
1605 N.W. 14TH AVENUE
GAINESVILLE, FLORIDA, 32601 U.S.A.
HARRY R. WARFEL, GENERAL EDITOR

REPRODUCED FROM COPIES IN

AND WITH THE PERMISSION OF

WESTERN RESERVE HISTORICAL SOCIETY

L.C. CATALOG CARD NUMBER: 66-11025

MANUFACTURED IN THE U.S.A.
TYPESETTING BY PEPPER PRINTING CO.
LITHOGRAPHY BY EDWARD BROTHERS
BINDING BY UNIVERSAL-DIXIE BINDERY

TABLE OF CONTENTS

INTRODUCTION

Richard H. Taneyhill's little book *The Leather-wood God* is valuable because it is the principal source of William Dean Howells's fine novel of the same name. It is also an authentic record of how in 1828 an imposter claimed to be God Almighty and promised that those who followed him would never die but live forever in the New Jerusalem he was about to establish on Leatherwood Creek in Guernsey County, Ohio. He won a sizable following that included some of the most influential settlers in the area. He said that his name was Joseph C. Dylks, that he could perform miracles, and that there was no salvation except through him. His teachings divided an entire settlement into hostile factions; neighbor often found himself pitted against neighbor, brother against brother, father against child, and husband against wife. Among the major prophets of Ohio in that era, Dylks was unique, the only one who pretended to be an incarnate human god. His battle with the Devil on the road to Marietta and his appearance before an Ohio magistrate in imitation of Christ's trial before Pontius Pilate make interesting reading.

Who Dylks really was and where he came from remain mysteries. He first appeared at a camp meeting not far from the present village of Salesville on a site on Leatherwood Creek, so called from a bush which grew along its banks. Before his advent, all of the settlers, most of whom were either Methodists or United Brethren, worshipped together in a common church, called "The Temple." After Dylks proclaimed his divinity, his followers seized this building, expelled the adherents of the older communions from it, and rededicated it to the new god. This highhandedness, of course, aroused opposition. Dylks's enemies arrested him and brought him successively before two magistrates, both of whom freed him, there being no law against a man's pretending to be God. The mob then forced Dylks to flee to the woods for safety. After the excitement had somewhat quieted down, Dylks emerged from hiding, called his followers together, and announced his decision that the best location for the New Jerusalem was Philadelphia, Pennsylvania. Soon afterward, the Messiah and three of his disciples—Michael Brill, Robert McCormick and Reverend Davis, a young United Brethren minister, turned Dylksite, — set out for that city on foot. Before arriving there, they separated, Dylks and Reverend Davis taking one road, McCormick and Brill another, with the understanding all should meet in Philadelphia. McCormick and Brill went to the spot agreed upon within the city, but neither Dylks nor Reverend Davis ever appeared. For days McCormick and Brill scoured Philadelphia but found no trace of either the minister or the Messiah. At length they returned, utterly discouraged and footsore, to Leatherwood.

In Leatherwood they found most of their co-religionists still firm in the faith, and before long both McCormick and Brill convinced themselves they had seen Dylks ascend to heaven. Their faith and that of the other Dylksites was greatly strengthened some years later when Reverend Davis appeared in Leatherwood and preached a sermon in which he, too, stated that he had seen Dylks leave the earth and disappear within the sky. Immediately after the sermon, however, Reverend Davis left Leatherwood and was never seen or heard of there again. Absurd as the stories of Brill, McCormick, and Reverend Davis were, the Dylksites continued to believe. As late as 1870 there were still men and women in southern Ohio who were waiting confidently for Dylks to reappear.

The chronicler of the great delusion was Richard H. Taneyhill, a capable lawyer, who lived in Barnesville only a dozen miles from the Dylksite Temple. Born in Calvert County, Maryland, Taneyhill at the age of ten, came to Barnesville with his parents. There he grew up, taught school, married Caroline Judkins in 1842, and read law. Admitted to the bar in 1847, he practiced law for several years in neighboring Noble County. There in the village of Olive in 1851 and 1852, he also edited the *Investigator*, a Whig newspaper. Presently he returned to Barnesville, where he served one term as mayor (1874-1876). He died on November 29, 1898.

Taneyhill was a born antiquarian. He loved to gather facts and to write about anything pertaining to the history of southeastern Ohio, whether Indian mound, ancient fort, or noteworthy personage. Among his numerous writings are two signed articles in J. A. Caldwell's *History of Belmont and Jefferson Counties, Ohio* (Wheeling, W. Va., 1880, pp. 187-191). The first is on Benjamin Lundy, the organizer of the first anti-slavery society in the United States; the second is on William Shannon, the first governor of Ohio to be born in the state. He also wrote the story of Logan, the Mingo Chief, for the *History of the Upper Ohio Valley* (Madison, Wisconsin: Brant and Fuller, 1890, I, pp. 37-46). His entertaining and valuable one-hundred-and-two-page *History of Barnesville* was published posthumously in 1899. In addition he contributed historical pieces, among them "The Leatherwood God," to the Barnesville *Enterprise* under the pen name of R. King Bennett. How many of these pieces he did is uncertain, as a fire destroyed the files of the *Enterprise* on January 12, 1895.

It is certain, however, that the first printed account of the Leatherwood God appeared in the *Enterprise* toward the end of 1869, for *The Guernsey County Jeffersonian* liked the story enough to copy it from the *Enterprise* (December 9, 1869; December 23, 1869; and January 6, 1870). Robert Clarke, the Cincinnati publisher, also liked the story and persuaded Taneyhill to revise and enlarge it for inclusion in Clarke's Ohio Valley Historical Series. There it was published in 1870

along with several other items in a volume en-
titled *Ohio Valley Miscellanies*. Clarke, however,
gave *The Leatherwood God* a distinctive title page
and paged it independently.

In a notice at the end of the *Miscellanies*,
Clarke stated that with this volume he was dis-
continuing the Ohio Valley Series because the people of the West had failed to support the Series
adequately. Nevertheless, over the years "a constant inquiry" developed for Taneyhill's narrative; in 1880 Clarke brought out a second edition,
this time as a separate work in pamphlet form.
There is no substantial difference between the
text of the first and second editions, though the
second edition is printed on smaller stock and runs
to 59 pages, whereas the first contains only 53.

For Clarke, Taneyhill made several corrections
and additions. The account in the *Jeffersonian*
is approximately 6,000 words long; that published by Clarke about 12,000. In the newspaper
Taneyhill said that community churches like the
Temple at Salesville were common in the West in
pioneering days. In the revision he said they
were rare. Again the book clarifies some details
in the newspaper's account of how Dylks bound
the Devil. Thus, Taneyhill wrote in the newspaper that, as Dylks and McCormick were traveling on the road toward Marietta, they met the
Devil who attempted to block their way but fled
in terror when Dylks gave one of his tremendous
snorts. The two men chased Satan until he threw
himself for safety into the body of brother Davis
where Dylks bound him fast "within it, not to be

loosed for a thousand years." No explanation of
how brother Davis happened to be on the scene is
given. The revised version is less confused. In
the book brother Davis isn't involved at all. The
Devil flees from Dylks and McCormick to the
house of brother Mason in Monroe County and
seizes Mason's son David, a man of twenty-five
who is ill with consumption. On the arrival of
Dylks and McCormick, David arises from his bed,
and hails Dylks as his deliverer, whereupon Dylks
binds Satan fast "for a thousand years" (p. 24).

Taneyhill was careful to state that much of
the additional material in the book was communicated to him by a Methodist minister, the Reverend George Brill, "then, as now, a resident of
the Salesville community and an eyewitness of
the facts he narrates" (p. 28). From Brill, Taneyhill learned what happened at the Temple after
Dylks failed to perform a promised miracle, how
Dylks was given two trials rather than one as the
newspaper reported, and how Dylks mysteriously
disappeared after his hiding place in the woods
was discovered. In general the book is better arranged and the narrative more coherent and vivid
than the earlier account.

Taneyhill's little book fascinated William Dean
Howells, who was born at Martins Ferry, Ohio,
only forty miles from the scene of the imposture.
Soon after the book appeared, Howells, as part
of his editorial duties on the *Atlantic Monthly*,
summarized it for that magazine (XXVIII [1871],
255-256). The summary gives a good idea of the
story, though Howells misdated Dylks's advent as

"about the year 1817" and confused the United
Brethren of the narrative with the Moravians, a
totally different sect.   Again, in 1897 Howells returned to Taneyhill's *The Leatherwood God* for
facts on which to base his account of the imposture in *Stories of Ohio,* a history book intended
for use in the schools of Ohio.   In this account
Howells's tone is appropriately more didactic than
it had been in the summary in the *Atlantic,* em-
phasizing the pitiful state of the self-deluded
Dylksites.   Howells was a compassionate man,
and by 1916 when he published his novel, *The
Leatherwood God,* he could even pity the wretched
Dylks, who, Howells was certain, must have come
to believe his own lies, a point of considerable im-
portance in the explanation the novel gives of the
delusion.

Howells, of course, transmuted Taneyhill's report into fiction.   He enlarged Taneyhill's brief
mention of a young woman who had become in-
fatuated with Dylks into a dramatic love story in-
volving Jane Gillispie, Jim Redfield, and Dylks.
He invented characters like Nancy Billings, the
deserted wife of Dylks; Laban, her husband; and
Joey, Dylks's son.   He telescoped the two trials
of Dylks reported by Taneyhill into one.   And he
vivified the background of the story with many
recollections from his own boyhood in the Ohio
Valley—the woods, the snake-infested swamps,
the cornfields, the tobacco patches, and the tumble-
down shacks where shiftless folk like the Rev-
erdys lived.   Howells's story is a work of art;
Taneyhill's narrative, a chronicle.   Nevertheless,

Howells's debt to Taneyhill was considerable, and
so he had the publisher state in a prefatory note
that in addition to many details, the verbatim report of Dylks's last words to his followers at the
Temple and the historical outline of the story had
been taken from "the admirable narrative of
Judge Taneyhill."

Could Taneyhill have read this note, he would
have strenuously objected to the title which it be-
stowed on him, because he hated pretense, and he
had never been a judge. On the other hand he
would have been gratified at having his narrative
called "admirable," for he was justly proud of his
contributions to local history. In general the
quality of his work is high; certainly his mono-
graph on the Leatherwood God would do credit to
a university-trained historian. He wrote it forty
years after Dylks's advent on Leatherwood Creek,
and he had to gather his information from oral
sources. He diligently sought out eyewitnesses,
and in an effort to be fair interviewed both Dylksites and unbelievers. His patient sifting of the
evidence led to the conclusion that it illustrated
how gullible people of average intelligence could
be. What particularly impressed him about the
followers of Dylks was the constancy of their
faith. In spite of the shabby way Dylks had
treated them, nearly all of them clung to the belief that he would one day return to establish the
New Jerusalem in their midst.

The power which the Dylksite delusion had
over these people is understandable in the light
of the conditions amid which they lived. They

were settlers in a new country. To them life must often have seemed a dreary round of backbreaking, monotonous, discouraging toil, unrelieved by books, music, the theater, or even organized sport. To these poor people Dylks brought a vision of a deathless life in a New Jerusalem, located not beyond the sky but nearby on Leatherwood Creek. There the faithful would live in fine houses, walk streets carpeted with green velvet, and ride in red chariots drawn by jet-black horses. Dylks was a wonderful talker; in that period of great religious receptiveness he might well have succeeded in founding a lasting cult, had he been able to perfect an organization. But, as Taneyhill noted, as an organizer, Dylks was "a mere bungler" (p. 43), and therefore his movement died out.

The story of Dylks and his followers is still current as a local legend in Guernsey County, where it has been passed down by word of mouth for several generations. Later research, however, has added little to Taneyhill's narrative. After nearly a century, his book remains an authoritative record of how far astray the religious frenzy which swept over the Ohio Valley in the 1830's and 1840's could carry intelligent but untutored people.

GEORGE KUMMER

Western Reserve University
March 30, 1965

NOTE

Sources for the life of Taneyhill include the obituary in *The Barnesville Enterprise,* December 1, 1898, and that in *The Barnesville Saturday Whetstone,* November 29, 1898. See also *History of Noble County, Ohio* (Chicago: L. H. Watkins and Company, 1877), pages 173, 179, 205-206; *History of the Upper Ohio Valley* (Madison, Wisconsin: Brant and Fuller, 1890) I, 729-730; and R. H. Taneyhill, *History of Barnesville* (Barnesville, Ohio: The Leatherwood Publishing Co., 1899), *passim.*

THE LEATHERWOOD GOD.

An Account of

The Appearance and Pretensions

OF

JOSEPH C. DYLKS

In Eastern Ohio in 1828

By R. H. TANEYHILL

———

CINCINNATI
ROBERT CLARKE & CO
1870

THE main facts of this narrative were published a few years ago, by Mr. Taneyhill, in a series of articles in the Barnesville (Ohio) *Enterprise*, under the *nom de plume* of " R. King Bennett." The various statements have since been verified, and the narrative enlarged by the evidence of other witnesses. The delusion of which it treats was so extraordinary in its nature, and produced, in so short a time, so great and permanent a change in the religious belief of so many intelligent persons, that we have thought it worthy of preservation in our " Miscellanies," as a curious episode in the religious history of the Ohio Valley.

Outline of Contents.

———

The Leatherwood God.

RELIGIOUS impostors have flourished in almost every portion of the historic period. Nor is this remarkable, when we reflect that man, universally, is disposed to give credence to marvelous stories, to put faith in sanctimonious pretensions, and to refer whatever he does not understand to some supernatural agency. These religious cheats have always found ready subjects to impress with their views, however visionary, and to mold into material to promote their ulterior schemes and purposes, however absurd and wicked.

Such an impostor was JOSEPH C. DYLKS, whose advent, teachings, journeyings, and unhallowed pretensions, are truthfully rehearsed in the following pages, and form one of the most interesting and curious episodes in the history of the Ohio Valley.

REGION WHERE HE APPEARED.

The settlement at Salesville, Guernsey county, Ohio, was begun in the year 1806. The settlers composing it were principally from the States of Pennsylvania and Virginia, with occasionally an immigrant family, who had ventured from the old world to fight the battle of life in the new.

The lands within the limits of the settlements were very rich, well watered, and heavily timbered. Through them flowed the Leatherwood creek, skirted by wide bottoms. Its clear, bright waters, sparkling amid copses and woods, fell sufficiently at various points to afford water-power for mills, while numerous tributary streams coming down from the hills, laved the banks of narrow, fertile valleys, and gave ample supplies of good water for man and beast. Springs were abundant, and the scenery at many points was picturesque and romantic. A region possessing such a variety of advantageous conditions was well calculated to attract to it, as this did, a class of settlers averaging above those of the majority of settlements in the Valley of the Ohio, in intelligence, morality, and educational advancement. Prominent among the early settlers here were the Brills, Frames, Williamses, and Pulleys, the numerous descendants of whom have contributed so much to make that neighborhood one of the most enlightened and refined in our great and beautiful State.

The settlers at Salesville were subjected, however, to the hardships common to the pioneers of the West. A wilderness had to be subdued, great forests had to be felled, and untamed nature to be reclaimed into fields and meadows. Houses had to be built, out-buildings to be constructed, and the infinite appliances of our civilization to be brought about them; all of which required time, and the exertion of much physical and mental labor. The settlers, therefore, had but little leisure to devote to the embellishments and charities of life.

STATE OF RELIGION IN THE SETTLEMENT.

At the pioneer settlements of the West, the families at any given point were generally of one religious creed, being drawn together by the reciprocal attraction of a common sentiment.

Salesville, however, was an exception. The settlers here were of divers religious views; some were Methodists, some United Brethren, while others represented many of the sects of the day. Nearly all were men of deep religious convictions, to whom the worship of the Most High was a necessity. Hence, as early as 1816, all united in a common effort, and put up a commodious, hewed log church, about the fourth of a mile north of the Leatherwood creek, on the hill overlooking the present village of Salesville. As it was the property of no sect, it was called by common consent the *Temple.*

At this house of worship, for many years, the settlers met regularly to offer up their devotions. But as ministers came among them only at long intervals to deliver religious instruction, that work fell generally upon some of themselves, and it was done with a will and force that caused the *Temple* and its worshipers to be a power in the land, wide-spread and influential.

Time wore away, during which the other settlements of Eastern Ohio erected church-houses, and the Methodist and United Brethren churches established circuits and appointed preachers to administer to the spiritual wants of the people; the *Temple* still remaining a common shelter for the worship of all sects, demonstrating that often-spoken, but seldom-practiced, expression, "How pleasant it is for brethren to dwell together in unity."

The ecclesiastical polity of the United Brethren church is very similar to that of the Episcopal Methodists. They hold general, annual, and quarterly conferences; have bishops, presiding elders, itinerant ministers, and local preachers. For ministerial administration they divide the country into diocese, districts, and circuits, the presiding elders and traveling preachers being supplied by the annual conferences.

LEATHERWOOD CIRCUIT.

At the time of which I am about to write, the Salesville congregation of United Brethren and the

Temple were included in what was called the Leather-wood circuit, which then extended from the Conauton creek, Tuscarawas county, to Marietta, and from the Muskingum to the Ohio river. It was called a circuit, although there was but little of the circle about it, as the appointments lay almost in a straight line from the Conauton to Marietta. There were eight or ten preaching places south of the *Temple,* and as many more north of it. The Annual Conference of 1828 met in March, and appointed Rev. John Crum presiding elder of the district embracing the Leatherwood circuit, and the Revs. Sewell Briggs and Abner Martin, as the itinerant ministers for the circuit itself. To be as near the center of his field of labor as possible, Mr. Briggs located his family with the *Temple* congregation, while his coadjutor resided at the north end of the circuit.

This conference year began with bright prospects for the United Brethren of the *Temple* neighborhood. Concord prevailed among the membership, zeal inspired their hearts, and a godly sorrow for sinners determined them to exalt Zion and to extend and establish her borders. The reverend gentlemen appointed to minister to their spiritual wants were deeply imbued with the spirit of the Gospel, and were ardent to confirm the brethren and sow the good seed that should "spring up to eternal life."

So in harmony and peace, in labors many, but with

reward abundant, the *Temple* congregation moved on
in their religious work through the spring and summer
of that year, until the month of August was reached,
when their Destroyer came—a destroyer that broke the
unity of the church, seized their *Temple*, and sup-
planted the faith of their fathers by the most audacious
and blasphemous errors, that ever found support in the
infatuation of enlightened men.

ADVENT OF THE LEATHERWOOD GOD.

About the middle of August, a camp-meeting was
held on the lands of one Casper Overley, two and a half
miles north-west of the *Temple*, in the immediate vi-
cinity of the M. E. Chapel, called Miller's meeting-
house, under the auspices of the United Brethren
church. The camp-meeting began on a Wednesday,
and was to continue over Sunday. On Sunday the at-
tendance was very large, the ingathering being from
over twenty miles around. The Rev. John Crum, P.
E., addressed the congregation at the afternoon service.
He had proceeded about half way in his discourse, and
by his eloquent appeals had obtained the profound attention of the audience, and had wrought their feelings
up to their intensest pitch; a silence solemn as the
quietude of the grave pervaded the congregation, when
a tremendous voice shouted " Salvation !" followed instantly by a strange sound, likened by all who heard it
to the snort of a frightened horse. The minister was

taken by surprise and stopped preaching, all eyes were turned to the spot whence the sound seemed to proceed, and were fixed on a stranger of odd appearance, seated about midway the congregation. He sat steadfastly in his seat, with a countenance of marked solemnity, and totally unmoved by the excitement which he had produced. That stranger was JOSEPH C. DYLKS, the noted "*Leatherwood God.*" The shout and snort of Dylks are described by every one who heard them as imparting to all within their sound both awe and fear. One who had heard them often said: "They carried with them, right through you, a thrill like that felt when greatly scared in the dark, and a dread similar to that experienced when we think of dying instantly." Their effects upon the congregation at the camp-meeting were singular indeed. Some of the men jumped to their feet, others bounced in their seats, women shrieked aloud, and every cheek blanched. It was several minutes before the minister could proceed with his sermon; but the people gave no further heed to it, they were too much absorbed in scrutinizing the mysterious stranger.

The strangest circumstance, however, connected with his advent is, that no one saw him come into the congregation, nor had any one there ever seen him before. The most searching inquiries were made, but no witness ever appeared to verify the manner of his com-

ing.   He was there, but that is all we will ever know
about it.

HIS PERSONAL CONDUCT.

The dress and personal appearance of Dylks were
such as to heighten the astonishment of the people concerning him.   He was about five feet eight inches high,
straight as an arrow, a little heavy about the shoulders,
but tapered symmetrically to the feet.   His eyes black,
large and flashing; nose, slightly Roman; forehead, low
and broad; hair, jet-black, long, and glossy, thrown
back from the forehead over the ears, and hung in a
mass over the shoulders, reaching nearly to the middle
of the back.   His face was fair, but pale, and was pervaded by a look of deep solemnity, tinged with melan-
choly.   He was dressed in a black broad-cloth suit,
frock coat, white cravat, and wore a yellow beaver hat.
He appeared to be between forty-five and fifty years of
age.   When we reflect that this was the day of linsey-
wool hats, hunting shirts, and wamuses; that there was
not in that large multitude one broad-cloth coat, and
not a male person whose hair was not cut close, and who
had not a rustic, pioneer look, we see, at once, how these
considerations complicate the question, how he got into
the congregation unnoticed.

SUBSEQUENT CONDUCT.

When the congregation was dismissed, of course,
many sought the acquaintance of Dylks.   He main-

tained a solemn gravity, but was affable and pleasant in his
manner to all who approached him. He was invited home
for supper by Mr. Pulley, at whose house he sojourned
for several days. Dylks attended the night services, and,
at the time most opportune for making the greatest im-
pression on the people, again gave his shout and
snort.

An advent so strange and mystical—so like the
coming of a spirit—was well calculated to excite the
credulity of the people, and to form a ready and sure
basis for the pretense that he was endowed with supernatural powers. He immediately availed himself of
the vantage ground given him over the minds of the
community, and began secretly to declare himself to be
a celestial being, bearing in his person a heavenly mission. Dylks was very sociable, and took great delight
in visiting from house to house. He was everywhere
received with hospitality and, kindness, and when he
bade adieu to a family, was always requested to repeat
his visit. This afforded him fine opportunities to carry
forward his plans. For several weeks following his
advent, however, he made no public promulgation of
his pretensions, but attended the various religious meetings of the neighborhood, conforming his conduct to
the occasion, and fervently uniting in the services.
Sometimes he lead at the meetings, at which times he
informed his hearers that he was only a teacher and not
a preacher even. His manner of giving public instruc-

tion was peculiar. He used only one hymn, that
beginning:

> " Plunged in a gulf of dark despair,
> We wretched sinners lay."

This he would line off a verse at a time, then
expound it, then sing it, and so on with each verse
until the hymn was finished. His prayers were pointed,
sententious, and short—rarely occupying over two or
three minutes, and always ending with the Lord's
prayer. His expositions of scripture were clear, terse,
and spirited; his illustrations, familiar but pungent.
He seemed to be a master of the Bible, unhesitatingly
and correctly quoting any portion of it necessary for
the illustration of his subject. This was Dylks to the
public. In secret, he was impressing certain members
of the community with a knowledge of his tremendous
spiritual powers. Telling them that he came into the
congregation at the camp-meeting in his spiritual body,
then took a corporeal one, and clothed it as they saw
him there; that he could disappear and reappear at
pleasure, perform miracles, and finally that he was the
true Messiah come to set up the millenium, and establish a kingdom that should never end; that he should
never die, and that all who should believe on him
should live forever in their natural bodies, and hold
the earth as an everlasting heritage; that his kingdom
would spread over the whole earth, and nothing but
holiness dwell therein; that his body could be touched

only by his permission; that not one hair of his head could be taken from him. And that with one shout and one snort he could strike out the universe.

PROMINENT CONVERTS.

Conspicuous among the number lead astray by the secret teachings of Dylks were Michael Brill, Robert McCormick, and John Brill. As they played a leading part in the Dylks' imposture, I will give them each a brief notice.

MICHAEL BRILL was the earliest settler at Salesville. He was born in Loudon county, Virginia, in the year 1763, and was consequently in his sixty-fifth year at the advent of Dylks. Mr. Brill had been a prominent member of the United Brethren church for many years, and his acknowledged piety gave him a wide influence in the neighborhood. He was well off, owning a farm of one hundred and sixty acres about a mile northwest of the *Temple*. His family consisted, at the time, of several daughters and one son—quite a boy. John Brill and George Brill, senior, who will be spoken of hereafter, were his younger brothers.

ROBERT McCORMICK was born in Ireland, and came to the Salesville settlement in the year 1820, as a school teacher, which profession he followed in winter for many years. He was a member and local preacher in the United Brethren church. His farm adjoined that of his father-in-law, John Brill. At this time Mr.

McCormick was probably forty years of age, and in the
full bloom of great intellectual and physical powers.
He had a fine education, and was versed in the ways of
men. Standing high in the church, of strict integrity,
having an unblemished character, popular with the people, his personal appearance and manners pleasing and
attractive, united to an intellectual force unusual in
such a community, and a will-power unyielding and
vigilant, Robert McCormick was a personage well
fitted for a leader, and, as such, became the champion
apostle of the Dylks' imposture.

JOHN BRILL was also an early settler at Salesville,
and at the advent of Dylks was about fifty years of
age. He was also born in Loudon county, Virginia.
Although he does not occupy a leading position in the
Dylks' delusion, yet such were his relations to certain
prominent characters in it, that this narrative would be
incomplete without giving him a special notice. He
was a member of the Methodist Episcopal church,
and was a class-leader when Dylks made his
appearance; which station he had held uninterruptedly
for over twenty years. He was the owner of a large
farm, possessed much other means, and was eminently
popular and influential. McCormick and James Foreacre, who will perform an important part in the career
of Dylks, where his sons-in-law — Foreacre living at
the time on Mr. Brill's farm.

PROGRESS OF THE DELUSION.

We have said that Dylks had, up to this time, carefully guarded from the public, as far as he could, what he had been teaching in secret. But by some means unknown, it had been reported that he had sa d he should never die. This report reached the ears of George Brill, sr., at whose house Dylks had made frequent visits. So when he came again, Brill said to him: "I hear that you say you shall never die." Dylks very dexterously slipped out of the difficulty. He raised his hands, exclaiming: "This shell will fall off," —then looking at Mr. Brill, continued—"I can endure strong meat, but must be fed on milk for a time." The sagacious answer led Mr. Brill to infer that the report had started from a too liberal conclusion predicated on the language of Dylks.

It was now about three weeks since Dylks had made his *debut* at the camp-meeting, and during this time he had made many proselytes to his claims, including many devout and influential professors of Christianity. His plans were now fully ready for the public promulgation of his pretensions, and events favored him. It was now Rev. Briggs' time to go to the appointments south of the *Temple* and preach, but he was suddenly taken ill, and it became necessary to obtain some other person to fill his place. Mr. Mc-Cormick was at last prevailed upon to make the tour in the place of the sick brother. He consented with the understanding that Dylks would go with him as his coadjutor. This Dylks agreed to do, and all things were made ready for them to start from the *Temple* on the next Wednesday morning.

The first three appointments south of the *Temple* were Seneca, which was near where Mt. Ephraim now stands, in Noble county, Ohio. The next was at the dwelling house of a brother named John Christhaven, some miles further south; and the third, at the dwelling house of another brother named Mason, who lived in the southwest corner of Monroe county. This brother, Mason, had a son named David, who was an invalid, and confined to the house by consumption. David was about twenty-five years old, and had been for a year or two a licensed local preacher in the United Brethren church.

Wednesday morning came, and McCormick and Dylks set forward from the *Temple* to administer to the congregations at the several appointments south of the *Temple.*

THE JOURNEY AND ADVENTURES OF DYLKS AND McCORMICK.

The following account of this clerical tour was placed in my hands by a gentleman whose father received the statements embodied in it from McCormick himself, which he reduced to writing at the time. The writer was one of Dylks' disciples, and placed implicit faith in what was told him by Mr. McCormick. Coming as it does from a genuine believer, who stood high in the Dylks' brotherhood, through an honorable source, I do not hesitate to pronounce it official. I give it entire, only changing a few words and giving it a few grammatical corrections:

"We had scarcely crossed the Leatherwood, when I seemed lifted up into a heavenly atmosphere. I felt extremely pleasant, indeed, full of joy. The face of Dylks grew brighter and lovelier; and his voice was exceedingly melodious. When we arrived at the top of the hill overlooking the *Temple* from the south, Dylks turned his horse's head, stretched out his hands toward it, and exclaimed:

"'Oh! how ignorant is that people of my true nature. But time will reveal all things to them.' We then went on, occasionally stopping to pray and to give thanks to God, arriving at Seneca in due time. At this appointment, we discharged our religious duties to the apparent acceptance of the congregation. But we did not go to bed until late, consuming the time in prayer, singing praises to God, and reading his word. Started early the next morning; when we had gone but a short distance a bright light circled the head of Dylks, who continued wrapt in thought for some time. When we stopped to pray as we had done the day before, this light remained over the saddle until Dylks would remount. So we continued to travel until we were

about half way, when he heaved a deep sigh and said:
'This work must be done.'

"We dismounted and prayed. This we did several times before we reached Christhaven's, the next
appointment. Dylks officiated there in a very satisfac-
tory manner. That night we did not go to bed at all,
but sat up praying and reading the Scriptures. From
the moment we left this appointment, the face of Dylks
got lovelier and his voice sweeter. About noon we
dismounted to pray. His countenance then appeared
as if he were in an agony of mind. Up to this time
whenever I was in Dylks' company, my feelings were
very agreeable, but now I was oppressed. The day had
been very clear—not a cloud to be seen—and the sun
shone bright and hot. But as soon as we remounted, a
chilliness, that almost made my teeth chatter, seized my
body, and continued until Dylks ordered a halt. Looking me steadfastly in the face for a minute or two, he said:
'Time is most precious now. We must stop praying.
Now is the time for work. I now reveal unto you,
that you are *Paul, the apostle.* You will shortly see
most wonderful things. I will increase your faith so
that you may see the sights of my power with understanding, and by them magnify my glory among men.'
As soon as Dylks begun speaking the chilliness left me,
and I felt more joyful than ever I felt before. Here
Dylks cast his eyes skyward, and remained motionless
a few minutes. The bright light of day suddenly be-

came as mere twilight, then it as rapidly grew light as ever again, when Dylks exclaimed: 'Did you not hear that sound—like the rushing storm. It was the Adversary of souls cleaving the air. I saw him sweep with hell-lit wings the top of yonder woods, and dart to earth to give me battle. Fear not, I will vanquish him.'

"We started on, and shortly descending into a ravine, thickly wooded, with steep hills on both sides of the road, when we saw the devil standing in our way. Dylks dismounted for the conflict, and exclaimed in a loud voice: 'Fear not, Paul; this done, my work is done.' With a firm and deliberate step, Dylks marched on to the combat. Satan did not flee, but prepared to meet him. He poised himself on his cloven feet in firmest attitude for mortal stroke; half lifted his flaming wings; bristled his scaly folds with sounds like muttering thunders; shot out his forked tongue, each prong streaming with liquid fires; rolled his glaring eyes which seethed in their sockets; while a hissing noise, terrible as the screams of the damned, bubbled in the throat of his majesty infernal.

"Dylks knelt and prayed, arose, shouted salvation, and blew his breath toward the enemy of mankind. The devil's wings dropped, his scaly folds recoiled, his tongue was motionless, and his eyes, appalled, stood still, and with leaps terrific, which shook the earth at each rebound, he fled the field. We followed with all the haste we could, keeping close upon him, until we came in sight of brother Mason's house, when the devil jumped the fence and sprang to the door. The door did not open, but the devil disappeared from us.

"When we entered the house, which we did without hitching our horses, we found brother Mason in, and his son, Rev. David Mason, lying on a bed. He got up from the bed as soon as we entered, and embraced Dylks as his Savior, remarking that the devil had taken possession of him, and that he knew Dylks as soon as he came in as his deliverer. Dylks then said: ' Let us pray.' We knelt, and Dylks prayed. When we arose from prayer, the house was filled with a strange, bright light, and every face shone with a lustre beautiful to see. Dylks then walked around Bro. David Mason three times, rubbing his hand against his body all the time, and saying: 'I bind the devil for a thousand years, not to be loosed to meddle in the affairs of men.' Having done this, he embraced David seven times, hugging him with much feeling, and then exclaimed: ' The perfect work is done.' Dylks then sat down. After we had eaten and rested ourselves well, I proposed to have our horses unsaddled, but Dylks said: 'No, we must return to the *Temple.* Preaching now is vain, useless—useless. There is now no salvation only by me.' I had no power in me to resist anything required of me by Dylks from that time on, so we bade the Masons good-bye and started home, where we arrived; how, you all know. Dylks talked but little on

our journey home, but continued to mutter to himself:
' The perfect work is done.'   Dylks never shouted salvation after his return, but simply snorted."

THE EFFECTS.

The unexpected return of Dylks and McCormick,
their marvelous story, and the public enunciation, now
for the first time made by Dylks, that he was the true
Messiah, come to set up a kingdom on earth, struck
the community with amazement.   This was intensified
into the profoundest astonishment, when it became
known that such men as McCormick, and Michael and
John Brill, with others equal in repute to them, and
fully one-half of the old worshipers at the *Temple*,
were believers in the doctrines of Dylks and firm
adherents to his cause.

The delusion spread with a rapidity scarcely ever
equaled in the history of religious fanaticism.   Family
was set against family, parent against child, husband
against wife, neighbor against neighbor, and so the imposture progressed, dividing and conquering, until the whole
church membership of the community were overwhelmed
by it, except George Brill, Sr., and James Foreacre.
They stood firm and unfaltering, the one a Methodist
and the other a United Brethren, the only remaining
pillars to sustain the old edifice of Christianity in that
neighborhood.   Around them the non-professors gathered to stem and beat back the wasting desolations of
the Dylk's delusion.   The Rev. Briggs was still sick,

and had to be an unwilling and helpless witness of the disruption of his church. His flock had wandered from the fold, and were gathered around a shepherd who promised to lead them at once into the New Jerusalem, and that, too, without encountering the King of Terrors.

THE TEMPLE SEIZED.

As nearly all the church members of every denomination had gone over to Dylks, they seized the *Temple* on the Sunday night following the return of Dylks and McCormick, and dedicated it to the use of the new dispensation. Dylks preached the dedication sermon. The brethren and sisters assembled in a body, and many others congregated, prompted by curiosity. At first, he was cautious in his language, but gradually grew bold, and at last gave utterance to the following blasphemous language: "I am God, and there is none else. I am God and the Christ united. In me, Father, Son, and Holy Ghost are met. There is now no salvation for men except by faith in me. All who put their trust in me shall never taste death, but shall be translated into the New Jerusalem, which I am about to bring down from Heaven." The brothers yelled: "We shall never die." The sisters screamed, Dylks snorted, and the spectators muttered indignant exclamations. The dedication ceremonies were converted into an uproarious religious tumult. Men shouted and yelled, women screamed and uttered prayers to Dylks to have mercy upon them, while he stormed and snorted. As Dylks descended from the pulpit, McCormick exclaimed : "Behold our God!" and the believers fell on their knees and worshiped him. When partial order was restored, McCormick announced that the next meeting would be held that night a week, and the congregation was dismissed.

The violent demonstrations of the Dylksites on Sunday night disgusted some who were wavering, and drove them back to the ancient landmarks, while they increased and confirmed the indignation and hatred of the non-professors. The lofty pretensions of the avowed God were soon put to the test. " We must have a miracle — some evidence of his stupendous powers must be produced—simple declamations will not do," were expressions every-where resounding in the ears of Dylks' disciples. He saw the necessity of some act to confirm his claims, and promised to make a seamless garment, if the cloth was furnished him.

A MIRACLE THAT WAS NOT PERFORMED.

Among the number carried away by the delusion was Mrs. Pulley, wife of him at whose house Dylks took his first supper in the neighborhood, as already mentioned. She was a very excellent and devout woman, and a prudent wife. She had just got home from the weaver's a piece of cloth intended for the winter's clothing of the family. This piece of goods,

as her husband was an unbeliever, she secretly conveyed
to Michael Brill's, at whose house the miracle was to be
wrought.   The people assembled at the appointed time,
eager and anxious to see the sight.   Friends were certain of its performance, enemies equally sure of a
failure.   Dylks delayed his coming.   Anxiety began to
take possession of the believers, and mirth to fill the
hearts of the "heathen doubters."   Much they looked,
and long they waited, but Dylks came not.   Nor did
the linsey cloth burst into seamless vestment under the
magic touch of the miraculous artificer, but remained
undisturbed in woof and roll.   And so ended the effort
at miracle.

Sunday night came, and a large congregation
assembled at the *Temple*.   The following account of
that meeting was communicated to me by Rev. George
Brill, then, and now, a resident of the Salesville community.   He is a son of the George Brill, Sr., here-
tofore mentioned, and a nephew of Michael and John
Brill.   Mr. Brill was an eye-witness of the facts he
narrates, and to him I am indebted for considerable
other information about the Dylks' delusion :

REV. GEO. BRILL'S ACCOUNT OF PROCEEDINGS.

"The *Temple* was crowded.   McCormick, who
officiated on the occasion, stood, as was the custom of
local preachers, in front of the pulpit.   Dylks sat
directly before him.   During his remarks, McCormick

alluded to Dylks as the 'Lion of the tribe of Judah,' and called him God. Dylks then sprang to his feet, and leaped into the air three times, giving vent to his peculiar snorting. He then cried out with a loud voice: 'I am God, and besides me there is no Savior.' This he did several times during the evening. McCormick continued, 'The day of salvation is past, the wicked shall be cut off, and we, the righteous, shall reign with Dylks a thousand years, with nothing to mar our peace or our happiness.' During the evening I saw several women go and fall down on their knees before Dylks and worship him. At the conclusion of the meeting, McCormick announced a meeting for the next Thursday evening, saying: 'When the old man, as you call him (meaning Dylks), will speak to the people.'

"Dylks now staid most of his time (continued Mr. Brill) at my uncle's, Michael Brill, who, with his family, were all firm believers in his pretensions, and so was my brother Christopher, who lived with his uncle Michael. Christopher once came over to my father's, and, with tears in his eyes, tried to persuade father and mother to believe on Dylks. Father told him it was all a delusion, but he left weeping, saying : 'Your damnation will be sealed.'

"During the time to Thursday night, many opinions were expressed about Dylks, and the excitement was intense. Some said he was crazy, others that

he was after money, a few that McCormick put him up
to it, but a large majority thought him to be what he
said he was.

"Before we went to the *Temple* on Thursday
night, McCormick came to our house. Father was
considerably aggravated at the shape matters had taken,
and was in no humor to hear any of the folly of
McCormick. He had not been there long, before he
began talking about the ' new faith,' and remarked to
father : ' I shall never see corruption, as I shall never
die;' and then said : ' Uncle George, you can not shoot
me.' Father sprang for his rifle, which hung on pegs
in another room, and would have shot McCormick in
the legs, if he had not begged off, saying : ' I was only
in fun, uncle.' There were a good many of Dylks'
believers there, on the way to the *Temple*, and it was
quite a damper on their ardor to see McCormick act
that way.

"The crowd at the *Temple* that night was great.
We could see them coming from every point of the
compass. Before we got to the house, McCormick
said : ' Dylks will not be out to-night, but I will fill
his place;' as much as to say, I am God! Some
person had started, for fun I suppose, a report that he
would be mobbed that night if he came out. The
Temple was crowded full, and nearly all eager to see the
Mighty God enter the church, but he did not come.

" Rev. Briggs went early, and sat down in the

pulpit with his head bowed down, so as to hide himself
from the congregation. Of the vast crowd, only one
or two knew he was there. McCormick took his seat
in front of the pulpit. All seemed to be anxious to
see what would come next, and a perfect silence
prevailed in the crowded house, when the Rev. Briggs
arose to his feet, as if he had been a specter, looked for
a full minute over the congregation, and said : ' This is
all a *fal lal lal.*' A scene followed that beggars description. The disciples of Dylks sprang to their feet, and
with one voice, as it were, cried out : ' He is my God ;'
and then left for Michael Brill's, where Dylks was,
shouting as they went : ' He is my God.' But a mere
remnant was left, as the followers of Dylks principally
made up the crowd.''

A REVEREND CONVERT.

The fame of Dylks had, by this time, spread
throughout the Leatherwood circuit, and had reached
the ears of the clergy in other fields of labor. Curiosity to see the pretender was excited in many of the
preachers, and one of them yielded to the temptation.
His name was Samuel Davis, a young man of fine
talents, and who had just been put into the itinerancy
of the United Brethren Church, in the north part of the
State. So he set out to see for himself this man who had
put himself in the place of God. At Wooster, Ohio,
he fell in with a young fellow-preacher, named Jacob

Brill, son of George Brill, Sr., who was in charge of
the Wooster circuit.   Brill was about to come home
on a visit when Rev. Davis arrived at Wooster.   So
they started for the Salesville neighborhood together.
Late one afternoon they arrived at the house of one
Heaps, a preaching station in the Leatherwood circuit,
near Antrim, Guernsey county.   Before they entered
the house Brill heard that Dylks was there.   He therefore cautioned Rev. Davis against him.   Davis replied :
" Bro. Brill, you need not give yourself any fears about
that matter."   They were introduced to Dylks.   After
supper Brill asked Davis : " What do you think of him
by this time ?"   " Think of him?   He's nothing but
a crazy old man," was Davis' reply.   " Beware, or he'll
have you, sir."   " Never," rejoined Davis.

During the conversations of the evening, Davis
seemed to give but little heed to what Dylks said, and
treated him with studied indifference.   The next morning, however, when Brill proposed that they start on
their journey, Davis said : " No, I shall not go now.   I
shall remain until Dylks goes."   Brill, finding Davis
had determined to stay, went on by himself.   In a few
days Dylks and Davis arrived in company at the Salesville neighborhood, stopping at Mr. McCormick's.   In
a short time thereafter, Davis announced himself a
believer in the teachings of Dylks.

ARRESTED BY A MOB.

Dylks' star, which had rushed to the zenith so rapidly, now began to wane. Enemies commenced to organize an opposition, and friends, when they saw that his lofty pretensions when put to the test, were only empty boastings, began to doubt. Having their plans perfected for the arrest of Dylks, they lost no time in putting them into execution. Mr. Brill's communication contains quite a graphic narration of the doings of the mob which arrested Dylks and carried him before the magistrates; and I transcribe it in full. Mr. Brill says:

"William Gifford, who lived in the neighborhood, had a daughter named Mary, a pretty and smart girl, about seventeen years of age. She was a believer in Dylks, and would listen to nothing her father and friends could say to her. She spent most of her time going around with the disciples wherever Dylks was. Gifford was a kind father, very fond of his daughter, and much distressed at her conduct; he entreated her with all his power to leave the delusion. She finally told him: 'If you will get me a single strand of his hair, father, I will renounce my belief in him as God.' Dylks had made them believe that this could not be done. Gifford resolved to have that lock of hair.

"James Foreacre, son-in-law of John Brill and brother-in-law of McCormick, was deeply mortified at their course, as he was a member of John Brill's class, and he determined to see if Dylks could not be frightened from the place, hoping by this to save Brill and McCormick.

"So, on a Thursday night, some weeks after the affair at the *Temple*, Dylks and some of the 'little flock' assembled at McCormick's. Dylks always called his disciples 'the little flock,' quoting that passage which reads: 'Fear not little flock, it is your father's good pleasure to give you the kingdom.' James Foreacre heard of the meeting, and got his brother John to go with him to McCormick's to help arrest Dylks.

"The same evening William Gifford attended meeting at Miller's Chapel, and there organized a company of four or five to go with him on the same errand that Foreacre and his party were about to endeavor to perform. But neither knew of the other's intentions. The Foreacres arrived at McCormick's first, went in, and tried to get at Dylks, but were driven out by the 'little flock.' John Foreacre then cut a club and said: 'I'll have Dylks or die in the attempt.' The Gifford party had now arrived, and as the Foreacres entered the house at the south door, they entered at the north. The 'little flock' was taken by surprise. My brother Christopher was of the 'little flock,' and he took a three-legged stool and got ready to throw it at them, when he thought: 'Why should I fight for God Almighty,' so he put the stool down and left, and gave up his would-be God.

"By this time, Dylks had slipped into the kitchen and hid himself in a corner by the chimney. Gifford sought him out, seized him by the hair of the head, and dragged him out of the house, and continued to drag him out through the yard. He tore out a considerable lock of Dylks' hair as a trophy to carry home to his daughter Mary. They had Dylks, but they did not know what to do with him. He made no resistance. Some one proposed to hang him, when Dylks trembled mightily. Another said, let's thresh him, and let him go. Finally, they concluded to take him before 'Squire James Frame, and see what the Civil Code provided for such fellows."

As Mr. Brill's account is silent as to what took place at 'Squire Frame's, I give it as I heard it from one who was an eye-witness.

BEFORE 'SQUIRE FRAME.

James Frame, the justice before whom Dylks was taken, was a son of Thomas Frame, one of the first settlers in that community, and a Methodist. The 'Squire was a man of good sense, and well versed in the statutes of the State. When the party reached the office with Dylks, they were soon informed by his honor that he had no law by which to try a "God." Thomas Frame, the father, was present in the room. After the justice had refused to take cognizance of the case, the old man stood a few minutes in silence, surveying the strange-looking personage before him, and then inquired: "Do you pretend, sir, to be God Almighty?" "I am God, and there is none else," replied Dylks. The old man remained silent several seconds, then extending both hands toward Dylks very solemnly said: "May the Lord have mercy on your poor soul." Dylks smiled and remarked: "The old man will believe by and by." Had Dylks remained silent, he would have been spared further trouble; but his wicked answer made the mob more furious than ever. So they bore him away to confront 'Squire Omstot, of Washington, Guernsey county, Ohio. This dignitary's office was located about where the Ark storehouse now stands in that village.

IN COURT AGAIN.

Arriving here bright and early in the morning, they awoke the public functionary from his slumbers to sit in judgment on the conduct of a pretended God. The morning was frosty, and the party chilled; but the 'Squire soon had his office aglow with warming flames, and they were ready for business. The specifications, charges, and statements of the accusers were duly presented. And now there came looming up new questions, grave and solemn, such as had never before been broached in the jurisprudence of his little court. Something must be done, but what should that something be? The 'Squire, having in finished style rubbed his "specks," and put them on his nose, took down the book containing the "be it enacted" of the General Assembly. With stunning look, he conned its pages, scanned the sections defining crimes; but, unsatisfied, turned his eyes beaming with fresh-born hope to the constitutional provision guaranteeing religious freedom; closed the book, and replaced it on the shelf; took off his "specks" and rubbed them again; threw a forlorn and despairing glance at the crowd, as if imploring pity for his miserable predicament, and subsided into a reverie, more perplexed and worse confounded than he had been before his reading. The suspense was terrible. How we are sometimes lifted unexpectedly to ourselves from the mire and clay of ignorance to the firm, broad highway of knowledge by the helping hand of some professional or literary friend. So it was with the 'Squire. A Cambridge lawyer happened to be in town, and after consultation with him, the 'Squire with eyes blazing with wisdom, and a mein bridled and reined with the starchy grace of judicial dignity, reseated himself. A 'Squire was of some consequence in those days. The crowd stood tiptoe, bending their bodies and shooting out their necks to catch the first sound of the magisterial thunder. The 'Squire spoke: "In this country every man has a right to worship what God he pleases, and that under his own vine and fig tree, none daring to molest or make him afraid. With religious fanaticism our laws have nothing to do, unless it be

pushed so far as to violate some of our public ordinances. This I find the prisoner has not done; he must
therefore go acquitted."

While the 'Squire was hunting the law, consulting
the lawyer, and pronouncing his decision, Dylks con-
ducted himself with fortitude and humility. When the
opinion of his Honor had been given, and before the
crowd began to breathe easy after the mighty strain on
their attention, the friends of Dylks, apprehensive of
violence from the Foreacre party, gave him a wink.
He sprang to the street and bounded up the pike, followed by his shouting accusers, who hurled at him a
shower of the recently broken stone that strewed the
road. Dylks escaped untouched, and was lost by his
pursuers in a woods which skirted the pike at the east
end of the village.

REIGN OF TERROR.

The Foreacre party, although foiled in the legal
prosecution, had gained a victory by putting the pretended God to flight, and so returned in triumph to
Leatherwood. Being now in the ascendant, if not by
numbers, yet certainly by the war spirit, they brought
the community under surveillance to their power.
The neighborhood was regularly and vigilantly patrolled; the houses of the "believers" put under strict
watch, and the entire region round about the *Temple*,
sleeplessly scoured by the scouts. Many were the

insults offered by them to the "faithful." Menace and
threat were indulged in so freely that the leaders of the
Dylks party desisted from all public demonstrations,
and quietly awaited the subsidence of the mob spirit.
Miss Gifford, having been put in possession of the lock
of hair, torn by her father from the head of Dylks, had
lost faith in the truthfulness of his Godship. A few
others deserted the faith, and it appeared evident to the
opposition that they had exploded the delusion. Dylks
not appearing, the believers remaining quiet, and the
indignation of the chief promoters of the persecution
having expended itself, the community settled to its
previous placid condition.

WHAT THE DYLKSITES WERE DOING.

Although the "believers," during the reign of
terror, had abandoned their public meetings and instructions, they were, nevertheless, sedulously spreading
the faith in secret. But no sooner had persecution
ceased, and active opposition ended, than they renewed
their public worship under the lead of McCormick.

Their number had not been in the least depleted
by the persecution, although a few had gone back to the
"herd of the lost," yet new converts had been made
sufficient to compensate for those who had gone astray.
Besides, the persecution had the same effect upon the
deluded that it always has had when directed against
religious fanaticism; it only intensified their faith and

strengthened their feelings of brotherhood. Their
public services were held sometimes at Michael Brill's,
sometimes at John Brill's, and at other times at the
Temple.

WHAT HAD BECOME OF DYLKS.

Dylks, who had disappeared on the run, had not
yet made his appearance, and what had become of him
was unknown to the "lost," as all were now denominated who rejected the teachings of the impostor. Many
were the stories invented, both by his friends and his
foes, about what had become of him. Some said he
had been taken by angels up to heaven ; others that he
was wandering about the neighborhood of the *Temple.*
Occasionally, strange lights were seen, and queer noises
heard, by some night traveler, and these were said to
be produced by the collision of Dylks' spiritual essence
with some Plutonian emissary come to torment the
faithful, but driven away by the timely interference of
their Lord and master. Another story, much circulated
at the time, represented that Dylks was seen in the
western part of Pennsylvania, near Washington, with
his face to the East, and walking very fast. The facts,
however, are that after he escaped from his accusers at
Washington, he made his way back to the Salesville
neighborhood. That while the terrors and vigilance of
the opposition lasted, he remained secreted in the
woods or out-houses, or at the obscure residence of

some believer little noted, having his wants supplied by his disciples. On several occasions he narrowly escaped detection and consequent violence by the indiscretion of his friends, who, when conveying him food, so acted as to excite the suspicion of the opposition.

AN ESCAPE.

At one time during the fury of the Foreacre party, the retreat of Dylks was ferreted out by three of them who were hunting him. They all had a plain sight of him, but he escaped in a manner unknown and mysterious. From certain actions of his disciples, it was suspected that he was hid in a thicket on the lands of one William St. Clair, who lived about a mile west of the *Temple.* Mr. St. Clair was one of his proselytes, and had, on several occasions, aided Dylks in eluding the pursuit of his enemies. The thicket was about midway between Michael Brill's and St. Clair's, and as both of these gentlemen were his warm friends, of course their houses and farms came in for a large share of the attention of the infidel mobocrats. The thicket was surrounded entirely by deep stagnant waters, except a narrow bench of land that formed a place of exit, but which could be readily watched by a single person. The three who were on the hunt of him entered the thicket on this narrow strip of land, and near the center of the area inclosed by the waters found Dylks sitting on a log. Fearing he might escape them, and to be certain of their game, they returned to the narrowest point of the passway through which they had entered the thicket, and posted two of their number as guards, while the third was despatched to inform their comrades. In a short time eight or ten others arrived at the point occupied by the guards. Leaving four of their number to watch the passage, the remainder marched into the circle formed by the guards and water, but after searching the grounds with all the care of men in earnest, leaving no place in which a human being could be secreted unexamined, they found no Dylks. He had vanished from their grasp.

DYLKS REAPPEARS.

Dylks was naturally a coward. For several weeks he had endured the horrors of great fear, and suffered an isolation as painful as an imprisonment. Nor did he permit himself to be seen by any but the faithful for a week or two after the opposition had disbanded their organization, and ceased to pay any attention to the disciples of the new faith. Fearing no longer for his personal safety, he made his appearance at a public meeting of the "believers" at Michael Brill's. He here exhibited great trepidation, watching every new comer with looks of suspicion, and keeping himself in constant trim for flight. He soon grew bold, however, and again began to visit through the neighborhood, extending them for several miles around the *Temple.*

FRESH DEVELOPMENTS AND AN ORGANIZATION.

For weeks following the reappearance of Dylks, divers meetings were held, and visitations from house to house carried on, the "brethren" strengthened, the wavering confirmed, and proselytes made and added to their numbers. Novelty, mystery, and miracle constitute the vital principles of every "new faith." And it is indispensable, also, that some of these be constantly active in the production of fresh developments to meet the emergencies of opposition, and to prevent the luke-warmness of the membership. Besides, members are nothing without an organization to bring them into order, to give adhesion to the individual parts, and to secure the permanency of the whole.

Dylks could not *do* the miraculous, but he could make promises stupendously novel, and could envelope his actions with an atmosphere of mystery. As an organizer he was a mere bungler.

But the time had now come when fresh developments must be made and an organization perfected. So, to accomplish these purposes, a meeting of the "faithful" was held on a Sunday night toward the close of October, 1828, at the house of Michael Brill. Rev. Davis, McCormick, John Brill, and many of the disciples were there assembled. Dylks announced to the brethren, that although the kingdom he was about to set up was to be on the earth, yet it was not of this world—was to be one of peace, harmony, and brotherly love. That as they had been met by violence, denunciation, and persecution, thereby subjecting them to much suffering for the faith, and that if he persisted in his work at that point, it was probable other outrages would be practiced upon them, and that as he did not wish to use force to carry forward the good work and establish the great city, he had determined not to bring down the New Jerusalem in that neighborhood, but had fixed on the city of Philadelphia as the point for its foundation. He also informed them that the time had fully come for the beginning of that work, to do which he must have his assistants, whom he called his apostles. He then revealed to the membership the persons who were to be his apostles: Rev. Davis was to be the "Peter" of the Dylks dispensation, and Michael Brill the "Silas," and that it would be necessary for them and McCormick, who was the "Paul," to go with him to Philadelphia, to assist in the establishment of the great city, which was to be the city of all cities, and was to fill the earth with its magnificence and glory. That during their absence, the "little flock" was to be tended by John Brill, who was to see that they met together once in each week for prayers and instruction. That when they prayed, the believers should keep their faces to the East, and he would not fail to remember them. That having erected the New Jerusalem, and made all things ready, he and his apostles would return, gather up the faithful, and transplant them in the midst of the great city.

Dylks, at the same meeting, presented his believers with a description of his New Jerusalem: "Its light would eclipse the splendor of the sun. The temples thereof, and the residences of the faithful, would be built of diamonds excelling the twinkling beauty of the stars. Its walls were to be of solid gold, and its gates silver. The streets were to be covered with green velvet, richer in luster and fabric than mortal eye ever beheld. The gardens thereof were to be filled with all manner of fruits, precious to the sight, and pleasant to the taste. That the faithful would ride in chariots of crimson, drawn by jet black horses that needed no drivers, and that their joys would go on increasing forever. That the air of the city would be redolent with the aroma of shrub and flower, while ten thousand different instruments, attuned to the symphony of heaven, would fill the courts, streets, temples, residences, and gardens with music ineffably sweet, swelling the souls of the saved with perpetual delight."

He informed his apostles that they must set out on their journey early the next morning. The question was then sprung as to money to bear the expenses of the trip, when Dylks remarked: "As for money, these," pulling three old rusty coppers from his pocket, "will be sufficient; for of them I can make millions of gold and silver."

THE JOURNEY TO PHILADELPHIA.

By times in the morning, those three devoted disciples of Dylks and apostles of his dispensation, Rev. Davis, McCormick, and Michael Brill, with their lord and master, started afoot from McCormick's for the city of Philadelphia.

They pursued their journey, sometimes by the highways, sometimes by the by-ways; at other times striking through fields and plunging across forests, scaling mountains without regard to roads, but always coming precisely to the ferries and bridges that afforded passage of the rivers and streams which lay in their way. How they managed to obtain food and lodging remains a secret to this moment. Dylks, however, so acted as to procure both. When they arrived to within about three miles of the city, the road they were pursuing forked. Dylks now said: "Faithful apostles, it is now necessary for us to separate for a time. Paul and Silas will take the south fork of this road, I and Peter will pursue the north. We meet again where the light from heaven shall shine brightest within the city, for there will the New Jerusalem begin to expand to fill the earth." They parted. McCormick and Brill went on, and in due time arrived at the city, but saw no light. They journeyed the city over, but still no light. Day after day they traveled the city, street by street, trembling between hope and fear, but still found no light. The light never came, nor did Dylks or Davis.

Having remained until the last vestige of hope vanished, with sorrowings and weepings, foot-sore and
moneyless, they set their faces toward Baltimore, where
they arrived in due time. Here, from the pledge of
their tobacco crop, which was still in the hands of a
commission merchant, they procured funds and went
home by stage. They made a truthful report of the
events of their journey, suppressing nothing. The
effect of Dylks' trickery upon the brotherhood was
scarcely perceptible. They had became too deeply imbued with the bewildering influence of the delusion to
yield it up, no matter what the defeat to their expecta-
tions might be, or how dastardly soever Dylks should act.
Illustrating that declaration of holy writ, that man may
be so far led away by delusion that he will believe a lie
to his own damnation.

DYLKS' SUCCESSIVE CLAIMS.

I have spent much time to gather together from
the statements of both friends and foes of Dylks, his
claims and pretensions, and the order in which he pro-
mulged them, with the arguments advanced to sustain
them. In so doing, I have carefully compared the tes-
timony, and have adduced from the evidence thus afforded me the following summary :

When Dylks first made his appearance in the
neighborhood of the *Temple*, he claimed to be only an
" humble teacher " of Christianity. Shortly, however,

he pretended to be the Christ of Calvary, returned to
resurrect the saints, and to set up the millennium.
While he was enforcing upon the believers this preten-
sion, he would often exhibit what he said were the nail
marks in his hands, the spear mark in his side, and the
thorn marks on his brow. Having established this
claim firmly in the minds of his disciples, he began to
teach that although Jesus Christ was a real Messiah,
had been crucified, and had arisen from the dead, yet
that he was not *that* perfect Messiah and Christ, vouch-
safed to man by the promise that: "The seed of the
woman should bruise the serpent's head," in that
"Shiloh" that was to "come," and in that Holy One
that was not "to see corruption." He contended that
that "seed," that "Shiloh," and that "Holy One,"
according to these promises, should never taste death.
So death should have no dominion over him (Dylks).
That if one died, so long as he was dead, so long
death held dominion over him. He said that death,
therefore, as a matter of fact, had had dominion over
Jesus Christ—had had a real triumph over him. That
the physical sciences demonstrated that a dead body at
the time of year in which the crucifixion occurred, and
in the latitude of Jerusalem, and dead, too, for thirty-
six hours, would necessarily within that time com-
mence to decompose, especially where the skin should
be broken. That in the mere article of death there is
corruption.

That *the* perfect Messiah and Savior should never taste death, but should be as immortal and immutable as the Father. And that he, Joseph C. Dylks, was that perfect Messiah and Savior, and hence should never die nor see corruption. After he had impressed these teachings upon the belief of his disciples, he assumed that this perfect Messiah and Savior must of necessity be God. And that he, Joseph C. Dylks, was the one only and true God—Creator and preserver of all things, and the finisher of man's salvation.

The time consumed in passing from one of these pretensions to another was short, as the zeal and infatuation of his followers made them ready to embrace and believe any thing he should affirm. Having taken the first step toward consummate blasphemy, they appeared anxious to reach it as soon as possible.

STABILITY OF THEIR BELIEF.

The firmness with which the followers of Dylks adhered to their faith is really surprising; for it is very doubtful, indeed, whether any one of them ever yielded up his belief in him as verily and truely God. Although death came and carried off one after another of the "believers," who, according to the faith, should never die, still those who remained were as unwavering in their belief as before. The church of the "old faith" was broken up, and could not be organized until new comers had accumulated in the neighborhood

in sufficient numbers to begin anew—the Dylksites
remaining by themselves, isolated and alone. And at
this moment, there is not one person living who gave
his adhesion to the " new faith," who is not as firm
now as he was then in the "faith." Those even who
were little girls and boys then, but now men and
women going down the declivity of life, are still looking for the reappearance of Dylks to establish the New
Jerusalem, and gather them within its walls.

THE RATTLESNAKE MAN.

The following incident illustrates how the children
were corrupted by the "faith." It was communicated
to me by an eye-witness of the facts related :

In the summer of 1850, a large man, about thirty-
five years old, stopped for dinner at the hotel of Mr.
Robert Mills, in Barnesville, Ohio. He was dressed
in an uncolored homespun suit, cut after the plain style
of the old Methodists, and wore his hair and beard long
and disheveled. He had a fine horse, saddle and briddle,
and on the valise pad was strapped a small flat box.
Having dismounted, he carefully unstrapped the box,
and carried it under his arm into the sitting-room of
the hotel. When invited to dinner, he took the box
with him, and put it on the floor by the side of his
chair. After dinner he brought the box into the
bar-room, and instantly inquired if any one wished
to see a rattlesnake ; if so, he would show one for a

dime apiece. A purse was soon made up. The stranger opened the box, and a large rattlesnake, having eighteen rattles, emerged from it and coiled itself on the floor. It was lively, and rejoiced to see its master; it shook its rattles, threw open its mouth, and shot ou. its tongue. The snake was fangless. One of the spectators seeing this inquired the cause.

"When I caught it, I took it up and knocked out the teeth with my jack-knife."

"Were you not afraid to take hold of it?"

"No; for had it bit me, it would have done me no harm. I shall never die; I shall live three hundred and fifty years precisely from this year, and shall then be transferred into the New Jerusalem without seeing death."

He then proceeded for over an hour to expatiate upon the claims of Dylks, saying that he had often seen him in the spirit—had frequent conversations with him; and he had been informed by Dylks that before the end of the present century, he should descend to earth and establish a kingdom of universal righteousness; but the building of the New Jerusalem would be deferred for three hundred and fifty years. The stranger gave his name as Moses Hartley; he resided in the mountains of what is now West Virginia. He lived in the Salesville settlement at the time Dylks made his advent, had seen, and heard him preach. He had just beer on a visit to the *Temple*, "the only place," he said, "where true religion had ever been revealed to man."

RETURN OF REV. DAVIS.

About seven years after the exit of Dylks near Philadelphia, the Rev. Davis returned to the neighborhood of the *Temple.* In the interval, the United Brethren congregation, recovering from the shock of the delusion, had put up their new church at the village of Salesville. Davis, who was well dressed, and looked as if he had lived sumptuously during his absence, boldly asked the use of the church in which to deliver a religious discourse. His request was granted, and at night he addressed the large congregation that came out to hear him for two or three hours. He there declared that he had seen Dylks ascend to heaven, and that he would shortly return to earth to set up his kingdom ; that Dylks was God, and that there was no true religion but that which recognized him as such. He denounced Christianity, saying: "It is only a hotchpotch of Judaism and heathenism." And that " the religion taught in the house in which I am preaching is as abominable as the car of Juggernaut or a temple for idols."

Davis left the next morning, and has never been heard of since.

DEATH OF THE APOSTLES.

Michael Brill died about two years after his re-turn from Philadelphia, continuing to be until death a sincere believer in the pretensions of Dylks.

Mr. McCormick lived for many years after the disappearance of Dylks. Throughout life he dressed much as Dylks did at his advent, wearing his hair so long that it hung below his shoulders. He died a few years ago an unflinching Dylksite.

Of the career of Dylks after his separation from McCormick and Prill near the city of Philadelphia, nothing is known. No reliance, of course, can be put in the stories of the Rev. Davis and Moses Hartley.

He came, performed his extraordinary part in the history of the Salesville church, set up his claim as the God of the universe, spread abroad his sacriligious teachings, gathered about him many followers, established a discord in the church at Leatherwood *Temple* which has not yet ceased, and then vanished. And this in all probability is all we shall ever know of him.

Reprinted from the Guernsey
Jeffersonian, Vol. 38, No. 31
Cambridge, Ohio, December 9, 1869

[From the Barnesville Enterprise]

THE LEATHERWOOD GOD.

His Advent.

BY R. KING BENNETT.

A neighborhood in the early settlements of the great West, had a much longer radius that that of the present time; sometimes reaching a distance of eight to ten miles. Yet, over this extensive scope of country, it often happened that there were but a few residents of any one denomination of christians. In such cases, being zealous for proper worship, two or more of these religious persuasions would unite their efforts and means and erect u church-house, careless about what kind of a preacher officiated, so that ke preached the gospel. The church-houses so put up by mutual combinahon, were used conjointly until numbers enabled each sect to employ a clergyman of its own faith, after which they were occupied by each at stated alternate times.

In the county of Guernsey, Ohio, many such places of public worship were built, and a few are still used there in that manner. The settlers at the neighborhood of the present site of Salesville, in Millwood township of that county, were nearly all members of the Methodist and United Brethren

Churches; but, each sect was weak in numbers. They. therefore, very early united in the erection of a church-house, about a mile and a half nor.h of the present village of Salesville, and about the same from the Leatherwood creek. This house was used by them conjointly and alternately for many years. And to their praise be it said, that it mattered not to them which sect the minister belonged, to they all came together to hear him preach. As population increased, the membership of these denominations gradually grew larger, so that it often happened, that the house could not contain the people assmbled. On such occasions if the season and weather suited, worship was held in an adjoining grove.

The inhabitants of the then Salesville neighborhood, were like those of the other pioneer settlements of the Mississippi valley. They were, generally, persons of sound, common sense, but lacking in the learning of books. And having the great forests to fell and farms to open up, they had only a little time to attend to intellectual pursuits; but, to the cause of religion and good morals, they gave earnest, constant and effective efforts. So that at the time of which I am about to write, the Methodists and United Brethern who worshipped at the old Leatherwood Church, had established over their entire community a morality and religous feeling excelled nowhere. And so in the faith of their fathers, and in the possession of that peace which its true practice produces, they were zealously, contentedly and com-

placently passing on the great process-
sion of life, when their disturber
came.

About the middle of August, 1828, a
two day's meeting was being held at
the old Leatherwood Church under the
supervision of the United Brethern
Minister in charge of the circuit. On
the first Sunday the congregation became too large to be accommodated in
the church, and a pulpit and benches
had been put up in the grove for the
use of preacher and people. The fore-
noon service was about half over, one
of the ablest of the United Brethern
Ministers was addressing the assembled multitude. The preacher warming up as he proceeded, had grown
very animated in his discourse, and the
people were giving deep and profound
attention to the sermon—a silence and
stillness—solemn as the quietude of
the grave pervaded the audience, when
a tremendous voice shouted out, "Salvation!" followed instantly by a
strange sound, likened by all who
heard it, to the snort of a horse much
frightened. The Minister was taken
by surprise and stopped preaching,
and all eyes were, in a moment, turned
to the spot from whence the sound
seemed to proceed and were fixed upon a stanger of odd appearence seated
about midway in the congregation. He
sat steadfast in his seat, eyes on the
clergyman, with a countenance of
marked solemnity, and totally unmoved by the many faces turned upon him
—by the shock of his queer interrup-
tion. That stranger was Joseph C.
Dylks, the noted Leatherwood God.

58

The shout and snort of Dylks are described by every one who heard them
as imparting to all within their sound,
both awe and fear. One who had
heard them often, said of them: "That
they carried with them right through
you a thrill like that when greatly scared in the dark, accompanied by a dread
similar to that experience when we
think of dying instantly." Their effects upon the congregation at the old
Leatherwood Church, were singular
indeed. Some of the men jumped to
their feet; others bounced in their
seats; women shrieked aloud; and every cheek blanched. It was several
minutes before the minister could proceed with the sermon; but the people
gave no further heed to it, they were
too much absorbed in scrutinizing the
odd stranger for that.

The strangest circumstance however,
connected with his advent is, that no
one saw him come into the congregation; nor had any one there assembled,
ever seen him before. The most
searching inquires were made but no
witness evei appeared to verify the
manner of his coming. Indeed, no
one could ever be found within the
State who reccollected having seen him
until that time. He was there, but
that is all we shall ever know about it.

HIS PERSONAL APPEARANCE.

The dress and personal appearance
of Dylks were such as to highten the
astonishment of the people concerning
him. He was about five feet ten inches tall, straight as an arrow, a little
heavy about the shoulders, but tapered symmetrically to the feet. His

eyes black, large and flashing; nose slightly women; forehead low and broad, and his hair jet black, long and glossy; was thrown back from his forehead and over the ears, and hung in a mass over his shoulders, reaching nearly to the middle of the back. His face was fair but pale, and was pervaded by a look of deep solemnity tinged with melancholly. He was dressed in a black broad cloth suit, and wore a yellow beaver hat. His age was about forty-five. When we reflect that this was the period of linsey, wool hats, hunting shirts and wamusses, that there was not in that large audience one broad-cloth coat, and not one male person but whose hair was cut close, and who had a rustic, pioneer look; we see at once how these considerations entangle with grave complications, the question how he got into the congregation unnoticed.

SUBSEQUENT CONDUCT.

When the congregation was dismissed, of course, many sought the acquaintance of Dylks. He maintained a severe gravity of looks, and carried out a commendable smoothness and deportment to all who approached him. He was invited home for dinner by a wealthy farmer, who immediately became inveigled by his artifices—Dylks attended the afternoon service. And at that point in its proceedings oppor tune for the greatest immpression, again gave the shout and snort with like effect upon the people.

An advent so strange and mystical, so like the coming spirit, was well calculated to excite the credulity of the

60

people and form a ready and sure basis for the pretense that he was endowed with supernatural powers.—
He immediately availed himself of the
vantage ground given him over the
minds of the community and began
secretly to proclaim himself to be a
celestial messenger bearing with him
a Divine commission. For several
weeks following his advent, however,
he made no public promulgation of
his pretentions; but attended the various religious meetings of the neighborhood, conforming his conduct to
the occasion, and fervently uniting in
the services. But, at each and all of
them never neglecting to give his ac-
customed snort and shout. While
these weeks were passing, he was busy
secretly impressing certain members
of the community with a knowledge of
his tremenduous spirtual powers. He
taught them that he had come into the
congregation in his spirtual body, and
had there taken to himself a corporeal
one and clothed it with earthly gar-
ments. That he was empowered with
indiquity, could disappear and reappear at pleasure; that he could perform miracles and was the true Messiah, come to set up a Kingdom or
righteousness never to end, that he
should never die, and that all who be-
lieved on him, should live forever in
their natural bodies and hold the earth
as an everlasting heritage; that his
kingdom should spread over the whole
earth and universal holiness prevail
among men; that his corporeal body
could be touched only by his permission, and that no one could by any

means, take a single hair from his head, and that he could sweep the universe into naught by one shout and snort.

PROMINENT CONVERTS.

Conspicuous among the number who were converted by the secret teachings of Dylks, were Michael Brill and Robert McCormick. As they played a leading part in the establishment and propagation of the Dylk's dispensation, will give each of them a brief notice.

MICHAEL BRILL.

Mr. Brill was a well to do farmer, owning a large farm, situated a little northwest of the present village of Salesville. He was at that time verging sixty years of age, and had a character eminent for christian piety, and possessed a wide influence. Although uneducated. Such had been his life that he held high official relations to the church of his choice and was greatly respected by all who knew him.

ROBERT M'CORMICK.

Mr. McCormick was, also, a farmer owned a farm and resided on it about two-and-half miles northeast of Salesville. He was about forty years old and in the full bloom of great intellectual, real and physical powers. He had been a member of the United Brethren Church for many years, and held the official position of local preacher when Dylks made his appearance in the neighborhood. Mr. McCormick had a fine education, was

versed in the ways of men and under-
stood human nature by intuition,
standing high in the church, of strict
integrity having an unblemished character—popular and influential with the
people—with a mind stored with vari-
ed learning—manners pleasing and
attractive—an appearance pleasant
and alluring, and united to an intellectual force rarely surpassed, and a will-
power unyielding and vigilant—Robert McCormick was a personage well
fitted for a leader, and as such, became
the champion Apostle of the Dyiks
imposture.

PREMONITORY.

The circuit of the United Brethren
Church, of which Leatherwood was
part extended from the Tuscarawas
river to Marietta, and from the Guernsey county line to the Muskingum.—
The interval between the times of
preaching at each appointment was
four weeks. During the time interve-
ning between the two days meeting a-
bove mentioned and the next regular
preaching day, a brother,——Davis,
who resided in the western part of
Washington county, and who was in
delicate health, paid a visit to the
Salesville neighborhood. He remained only a few days and returned home
—(My readers will pleas bear this fact
in mind, as it will become important
directly.)

By this time Dyiks had succeeded
in converting many by his secret
teachings, and had his plans complet-
ed, for a public avowal of his arro-
gant pretensions, lacking only an op-
portunity for their consumation.—

Events favored him: for, when the regular preaching day came, the minister suddenly took sick and was unable to go on to his other appointments southward. Looking about him for a substitute, he finally made choice of Robert McCormick, who chose Dylks as his coadjutor, with the approbation of the regular minister. So appointed, on the next day they set forward on their clerical journey, expecting to be absent for over a week. But, on the third day they returned with an account of the extraordinary and startling events they had witnessed, or, in which they had taken a part.

[TO BE CONTINUED].

Reprinted from the Guernsey
Jeffersonian, Vol. 38, No. 33
Cambridge, Ohio, December 23, 1869

[From the Barnesville Enterprise.]

THE "LEATHERWOOD GOD."

The Adventures and Journeys of Dylks and McCormick—An Official Account.

BY R. KING BENNETT.

The following account of their clerical tour and adventures was placed in
my hands by a very clever gentleman,
son of him who received the statements
embodied in it from McCormick himself, and by him reduced to writing at
the time. The writer was one of Dylks'
disciples, and placed implicit faith in
what was told him by Mr. McCormick.
Coming as it does from a genuine believer, who stood high in the confidence
of the Dylks brotherhood, through an
honorable source, I do not hesitate to
pronounce it official. It is only slightly
condensed; and wherever quotation
marks are used, the language of the
paper is faithfully transcribed:

They journeyed on towards Marietta,
the first day "occasionally stopping to
pray and give thanks to God." Put up
at night at the house of a brother. "But
did not go to bed until late, consuming
the time in prayer, singing praises to

God and reading His word." Started
early the next morning, acting during
the day as they had done on the day
previous, until about noon, when Dylks
ordered a halt. "Looking steadfastly
in the face of McCormick for a few minutes, Dylks said: 'I now reveal unto
you that you are Paul the Apostle. You
will shortly see most wonderful things.
I will increase your faith so that you
may see the sights of my power with
understanding, and by them magnify
my glory among men.' Dylks here
cast his eyes skyward and remained
motionless a few minutes, and then exclaimed: 'Did you not hear that sound
—like the rushing storm? It was the
adversary of souls cleaving the air. I
saw him sweep with hell-lit wings the
top of yonder woods and dart to earth
to give me battle. Fear not, I will
vanquish him.' "

Starting on, they descended into a
ravine, thick wooded, with steep hills
on both sides of the road, where they
beheld the Devil, blocking up their way.
"Dylks dismounted for the conflict,
and exclaimed in a loud voice: 'Fear
not, Paul; this done, my work is done.'
With a firm and deliberate step, Dylks
marched on to the combat." The Devil
was not unmindful of his antagonist.
He poised himself on his cloven feet in
the firmest attitude for mortal stroke,
half lifting his flaming wings—bristled
his scaly folds with sounds like muttering thunders—shot out his forked
tongue, each prong streaming with
liquid fires; rolled his glaring eyes
which settled in their sockets, while a
hissing noise, terrible as the scream of
the damned, bubbled in the throat of

66

his majesty infernal."

Dylks knelt and prayed—arose,
shouted salvation and gave his snort.
The Devil's wings drooped—his tongue
was motionless; and his eyes, appalled,
stood still, and with leaps terrific which
shook the earth at each rebound, he
fled the field. Dylks and McCormick
at the wiriest metal of their steeds
gave chase. The pursuit was continued until the Devil threw himself, for
safety, into the body of brother Davis.
Dylks and McCormick then, with many
prayers, much singing, and a great
deal of squeezing of brother Davis'
body, "bound the devil fast within it
not to be loosed for a thousand years,
to meddle in the affairs of men" Hav
ing taken refreshments, their horses
were brought out, when McCormick
proposed to go on to their appointments; but Dylks protested against
doing so, saying, "It is useless; there
is now no salvation only by me. We
must return to the temple, (meaning
the Leatherwood church), and set up
my kingdom." McCormick yielded to
his master's will, and they started home,
where they arrived, as we have already
stated. Dylks never afterwards shouted
salvation; but simply snorted.

THE EFFECTS.

The unexpected return of Dylks and
McCormick, their marvellous story,
and the public announcement, now
for the first time made by Dylks, that
he was the true Messiah, come to set
up a kingdom on earth, struck the
community with amazement. This was
intensified into the profoundest astonishment when it became known that

such men as McCormick, Michael Brill and John Brill, with others equal in repute with them, and fully one-half of the old worshippers at the Leatherwood church, were believers in the doctrines of Dylks, and firm adherents to his cause.

The delusion spread with a rapidity scarcely ever equalled in the h story of religious fanaticism. Family was set against family—parent against child—husband against wife—neighbor against neighbor, and so on the imposture proceeded, dividing and conquering, until the whole church membership of the community were overwhelmed by it, excepting George Brill. He stood firm and unfa'tering, the only pillar remaining to sustain the old faith of Christianity. Around him the non-professors gathered to stem and beat back the wasting desolations of the Dylks imposition.

The minister who had sent them out to fill his appointments had been unable to return home, and so remained an unwilling but helpless witness of the disruption of his church. His flock had wandered from the fold, and were gathered around a shepherd, who was to lead them at once into the New Jerusalem, and that too without encountering the King of Terrors.

The members having gone over in a body to Dylks, the Leatherwood church was taken possession of by them, and in it no worship was allowed save that of the new dispensation

DEDICATION OF THE TEMPLE.

About a week after its seizure the old Leatherwood church was dedicated by Dylks, as the temple of the new religion. The time chosen for that purpose was night, and it proved to be a crisis occasion in the destiny of the imposture. The brethren and sisters assembled in a body, and many others congregated, prompted thereto by curiosity. Dylks, McCormick and Brill occupied the pulpit; the disciples sat next to the pulpit, leaving the remainder of the room for the non-professors. Dylks began the services in the usual manner of public worship, took his text and proceeded to make known the purposes of his mission. He had not been speaking long when he used the following blasphemous language: "I am God, and there is none else. I am God and the Christ united. In me, Father Son and Holy Ghost are met. There is now no salvation for men only by faith in me. All who put their trust in me, shall never taste death, but shall be translated into the New Jerusalem, which I am about to bring down from Heaven." The brothers yelled, "We shall never die." The sisters screamed, Dylks snorted, and the spectators muttered indignant exclamations. The consecration ceremonies were converted into an uproarious religious tumult; men shouted and yelled; women screamed and uttered prayers to Dylks to have mercy on them, while he stormed and snorted As he descended from the pulpit, McCormick exclaimed, "Behold our God!" when the believers all fell on their knees and worshipped him. The feelings of the infidel spectators may well be imagined. In a short time these feelings took unto themselves the

form of action. At first, to test the
pretended powers and impious claims
of Dylks, they demanded of him the
performance of a miracle. This he
agreed to do by making a seamless
garment if the cloth should be fur
nished him.

Now, among the number carried
away by the delusion, was a Mrs. Pully,
a very excellent and devout woman.
She had just got home from the
weaver's a piece of cloth intended for
the winter's wear of the family. This
piece of goods, as her husband was an
unbeliever, she secretly conveyed to
Michael Brill's, the place at which the
miracle was to be wrought. The people at the appointed time assembled,
but Dylks make default, much to the
chagrin of his followers. From this moment Dylks' star, which had reached its
zenith with such a rush of success, began to be hurried to its fall. Enemies
thickened about him—friends doubted,
and his lofty pretentions when put to
the trial, became exposed as vain
boastings. The indignation of Mr.
Pully was so great when he heard what
his wife had done, that he threatened
v,olence to Dylks, if he ever laid eyes
on him.

A young lady, Miss Foreacre, pos
sessed of great beauty and quite intel
ligent, and who was the adoration of
her father, had been carried away by
the delusion. The furious demonstra
tions at the Temple had nearly crazed
her. Her friends expostulated with
her. Her father begged her to aban-
don the faith, but all in vain. Finally
she said to her father. "Father, if
you will get me only a single hair from

70

the head of Dylks, I will give up my
faith in him." Mr. Foreacre instantly
determined if he could find assistance,
to procure a lock of hair from the scalp
of the pretender. Meeting with
Pully, he stated to him his intentions,
and they solemnly averred to stand by
each other and give aid and comfort
to any project to put an end to the
imposture.

CIVIL AUTHORITY INVOKED.

A party was soon organized to seize
Dylks and take him before magisterial
authority. Dylks being apprised of
their intentions, eluded them for some
time. While this time was passing, a
Rev. Davis, a young clergyman of the
United Brethren Church, was dis
patched from the north part of the
circuit to fill the appointments of the
regular minister. When at the Win-
chester Station, he heard of the Dylks
excitement at Leatherwood, and repre-
hended the whole affair in the severest
language. In due time he arrived at
the house of Mr. McCormick, where
Dylks had taken refuge from the
Foreacre party. Davis had been at
Mr. McCormick's only a few days
until he became a convert, embracing
the entire claims of Dylks, with a zeal
equaled only by that of McCormick
himself.

THE SEIZURE.

By this time the Foreacre party had
discovered the retreat of Dylks, and
came down on him in the night, seized
him roughly and handled him afterwards without delicacy in the touch.
Mr. Foreacre, in order to save his
daughter from her infatuation, en-

71

twined his hand in Dylk's hair, and
snatched away a handful and thrust it
in his pocket. Having administered
severe rebukes to Davis and McCormick and confirming them with terrible
threatenings, the party secured Dylks
and hurried him away to confront his
honor, Esq. Omstot, of Washington,
Guernsey County, Ohio. This dig-
natary's office was located about where
the Ark Store-house now stands in
that village.

IN COURT.

Arriving here bright and early in
the morning, they awoke this public
functionary from his slumbers to set in
judgement on the conduct of a pretended Messiah. The morning was
frosty and the party chilled, but the
'Squire soon had his office aglow with
warming flames, and they were ready
for business. The specifications,
charges and statements of the accusers
were duly presented. And now there
came looming up new questions—
grave and solemn—such as had never
before been broached or mooted in the
jurisprudence of his little court.—
Something must be done, but should
that something be? The 'Squire having, in finished style, rubbed his
"specks" and put them on his nose,
took down the book containing "be-it
enacted" of the General Assembly.
With stunning look he conned its pages, scanned the sections defining
crimes; but, unsatisfied, turned with
eyes beaming with fresh-born hope to
the constitutional provision guaran
teeing religous freedom, closed the
book and replaced it in the shelf, and

took off his "specks" and rubbed them
again; threw a forlorn and despairing
glance at the crowd, as if imploring
pity for his miserable predicament,
subsided into reverie, more perplexed
and worse counfounded than he had
been before his reading. The suspense was terrible! How we are sometimes lifted unexpectedly to ourselves,
from the mire and clay of ignorance,
to the firm, broad highway of knowledge, by the helping hand of some professional or literary friend   So it was
with the 'Squire, A Cambridge lawyer happened to be in town, and after
consultation with him, the 'Squire,
with eyes blazing with wisdom, and a
mein bridled and reined with the
starchy grace of judicial dignity, reseated himself. An Esquire was of
some consequece in those days. The
crowd stood tip-toe, bending their
bodies and shooting out their necks
to catch the first sound of the magisterial thunder. The 'Squire spoke :
"In this country every man has a
right to worship God, under his own
vine and fig tree, none daring to molest or make him afraid. With religious fanaticism, our laws have nothing
to do, unless it be pushed so far as to
violate some of our public ordinances.
This I find the prisoner has not done ;
he must, therefore, go acquited."
   D· lks, who had, throughout, con-
ducted himself with gaeat fortitude and
humility, here received a wink from
his friends who were apprehnensive of
the wrath of the Foreacre party. He
sprang to the street and bounded up
the pike, followed by his shouting accusers, who hurled at him a shower of

the recently broken stone that strewed the road. Dylks escaped untouched, and lost his pursuers by dexterous dodgings, in a woods that skirted the road at the east end of the village. And so ended the judicial farce.

[TO BE CONTINUED.]

Reprinted from the Guernsey
Jeffersonian, Vol. 38, No. 34
Cambridge, Ohio, January 6, 1870

[From the Barnesville Enterprise.]

THE "LEATHERWOOD GOD."

BY R. KING BENNETT.

(Concluded)

SUBSEQUENT CONDUCT OF THE FORE-ACRE PARTY

The Foreacre party, although
foiled in the legal prosecution, had
gained a victory by putting the pretended Messiah to flight and re
turned in triumph to Leatherwood.
Being now in the ascendant, they
brought the community under surveillance to their authority. The
nieghborhood was regularly and
vigilantly patrolled; the houses of
the "believers" were put under
strict watch and the entire region
round-about sleeplessly scoured by
scouts. But Miss Foreacre having
seen the hair that her father had
secured from the head of Dylks
renounced the faith. Mrs. Pully
also recanted, and one or two others deserted the cause. The mo-
tive power, which had created and
kept up the indignation of the opposition leaders, Mr. Foreacre and
Mr. Pully, having been by these

means removed, they became luke-
warm, and the persecution abated
in fury, and finally at the end of
about three weeks ceased alto-
gether.

WHAT THE DYLKSITES WERE DOING.

The Dylksites, the name which
had now irrevocably fixed itself on
the disciples of the new faith, who
had, during the reign of terror, desisted from any public meetings or
teachings, but were watchfully
spreading the secret, commenced
once more to hold public worship
under the lead and instructions of
Mr. McCormick. Their number
had not been in the least depleted
by the persecution; although a few
had gone back to the "herd of the
lost," yet new converts had been
made sufficient to compensate for
the estrayed. Besides, the persecu-
ting efforts of the opposition had
the same effect upon the deluded
which such actions have always
had when directed against religious
fanaticism; they only intensified
their faith and deepened their feelings of brotherhood Their public meetings were held, sometimes
at the house of Michael Brill, sometimes at that of John Brill, and at
other times at the Temple. Had
Dylksism continued to be subject

to the leadership of McCormick, it
would have had a prosperous time
for years, but another fate awaited
it.

WHERE WAS DYLKS?

Dylks, who disappeared on the
run, had not yet again made him
self visible, and what had become
of him was totally unknown to the
"lost" as all were now denominated
who rejected the teachings of the
Imposter. Many stories were in
vented by both friends and foes
about what had become of him.
Some said he had been taken by
angels up to Heaven; others that
he was wandering about the neighborhood of the Temple in his spir
itual body. Occasionally strange
lights were seen and queer noises
heard, and these were said to be
produced by the collision of his
spiritual essence with some pluton-
ion emissary from hell to torment
the faithful; but driven away by
the timely interference of their lord
and master. Another story represented that Dylks was seen in the
State of Pennsylvania, face to the
eas', walking very fast. The facts,
however, are, that after his escape
from his accusers at Washington,
he made his way back to the Salesville neighborhood, and while the

terrors and vigilance of the persecution lasted, he remained secreted
in the woods or out houses, or at
the obscure residence of some little
noted believer, having his wants
amply provided for by his disciples.
On several occasions he narrowly
escaped detection and consequently violence by the incaution of his
friends, who, when taking him
food, acted so as to excite the sus
picion of the opposition that Dylks
was about. At another time his
hiding place really became known
to some of the Foreacre party; but
when they surrounded it and drew
in their lines. Dylks was gone,
having been removed to a place of
safey by some unbelievers who
discountenanced mobocracy, even
when applied to a false teacher.

RE-APPEARS

Dylks was a natural coward.
Fearing no longer for his personal
safey, he finally made his appearance at a public meeting which assembled at Michael Brill's. Rev.
Davis, McCormick and John Brill,
were among the number. Dylks
then announced, that as the brethern had been subjected to great
sufferings for the faith, and as he
did not wish to use force to vindi-
cate his claims, and as this he knew

would have to be done if he made further efforts in that neighborhood, he had determined not to bring down the New Jerusalem at that place; but had fixed on the City of Philadelphia as the final point for its foundation. He also informed them that the time had fully come to reveal to certain of the membership, their apostolic character, and that it would be necessary for those Apostles to go with him, to assist in the establishment of the great city, which was to be the city of all cities, and was to fill the earth with its magnificence and glory. He presented to them a description of his New Jerusalem. "Its heighth should eclipse the splendor of the sun. The temples thereof and the residences of the faithful should be built of diamonds, excelling the twinkling beauty of the stars. Its walls were to be of solid gold, and the gates silver. The streets were to be covered with green velvet richer in fabric and lustre than human eye had ever beheld. The gardens thereof were to be filled with all manner of fruits precious to the sight and pleasent to the taste. That the faithful should ride in chariots of crimson, drawn by jet

black horses that need no drivers;
and that their joys would go on increasing forever; that the air of
the city should be redolent with
the aroma of both flower and shrub,
while ten thousand different instruments attuned to the symphony of
Heaven, should sweep courts, temples, streets, residences and gardens with music ineffably sweet,
swelling the souls of the redeemed
with perpetual delight." He as-
sured his followers that so soon as
the city should be fitted up, he
would gather his disciples together
and usher them into its possession

My readers who are well acquain-
ted with theological literature, will
perceive that this description of his
New Jerusalem is simply an inco-
herant medley of the descriptions
given by other imposters of their
brave, with a faint resemblance
in one or two respects to the New
Jerusalem of St. John.

He then informed Rev Davis
that he was to be the Peter of the
Dylks dispensation, and Michael
Brill the Silas; and that they and
McCormick, who was the real Paul
of ancient times, should go with
and aid him in the erection of the
great city. As for money to bear
expenses, he said as he pulled three

old rusty coppers from his pocket, 'These will be sufficient, for of them I can make millions of gold and silver."

Preparations were made immediately for the journey, and on the morrow these three devoted disciples of the Dylks faith and Apostles of his dispensation, with their lord and master, started afoot for the city of Philadelphia. They pursued their journey, sometimes following the highways, sometimes the by-ways, and at other times striking through fields and plunging across forests: scaling mountains, never before crossed by civilized man—but always managing to hit precisely the ferries and and bridges that afforded passage of the rivers and creeks that lay in their way. How they arranged to procure food and lodging remains a secret to this day. Dylks so acted as to provide both.— When they arrived at a point about three miles from the city their road forked. Here Dylks made known to them that it was necessary for them now to seperate. Dylks and 'Davis were to take the north fork, and Brill and McCormick the south and were to meet at a designated point within the city, at which the been broken down, and so continued for about two years, when it began to recover from the effects of the Dylks imposture; or, more accurately speaking, new comers had moved into the neighborhood in sufficient numbers to begin church organization again: for only four or five of Dylk's disciples ever recanted the faith.

Mr. Brill died about twelve years afterward, continuing to be until death a sincere believer in the Messiahship of Dylks.

Mr. McCormick lived for many years after the disappearance of Dylks. Through life he dressed much as Dylks did at his advent, wearing his hair so long as to fall over his shoulders. He died a few years ago, an unflinching Dylksite. A few are still living who were lead away by the delusion, and are up to this moment zealous adherents to the claims of the Leatherwood God. This is indeed remarkable, when we remember that one of the cardinal doctrines of Dylksism was that none of his followers should taste death, and yet so many of them and their neighbors, too, have passed down to the valley of shadows.

RETURN OF REV. DAVIS.

About seven years after the exit

New Jerusalem was to be set up
They parted; Brill and McCormick went to the place agreed upon for their coming together
again, but Dylks and Davis never
appeared. Having remained a few
days, and Dylks and Davis still not
appearing, they, disappointed, sor-
rowing and footsore, set their faces
towards Baltimore, where they arrived in due time. Here, from the
proceeds of their tobacco which
was still in the hands of a commission merchant, they procured funds
and went home. They made truthful statements of the events of
their journey, suppressing nothing
The effect upon the brotherhood
was scarcely perceptible. They
had become too deeply imbued
with the spirit of the delusion to
yield it up, no matter what the defeat to their hopes might have
been.

The church of the old faith had
of Dylks, and after the United
Brethren Congregation had put up
their new church house at the vi'-
lage of Salesville, the Rev. Davis
returned to that neighborhood and
asked the use of the house in which
to deliver a religious discourse.
Now, it is a rigid rule of this denomination of christians to freely

give the use of their places of worship to the ministers of all other
creeds. This rule, so beautifying
to christian character, and the neg-
lect of which has so moved and bro
ken down the fellowship of the va
rious sects, was constructed on this
occasion with a generous liberal
ity and his request granted. He
thereupon harangued the people
for two or three hours. He there
declared that he saw Dylks ascend
to Heaven, but would shortly return to set up his kingdom, and
that here was no true religion
only that taught by Dylks. Chris
tianity he denounced, saying: It
was only a hotchpot of Judaism
and Heathenism, that the house in
which he was preaching was as
abominable in the sight of God, as
the Car of Juggernaut or a temple
of Idols.

FAITH OF THE DYLKSITES.

The most marked peculiarity of
the disciples of Dylks, was the
firmness and constancy of their
faith. Only four or five persons
of the many entangled in the delusion ever abandoned it. Through
evil and through good report they
were steadfast in the faith. Although sneered and scoffed at by
the world—persecuted above meas-

ure, deceived by Dylks often, and finally abandoned by him in a manner certainly disreputable in one pretending so much; they remained unwavering and unyielding in their devotion to his cause. And even now there are scattered about over the States men and women who have become grey-headed with age—who were then little boys and girls, in which the light of intellect had scarcely dawned, but were taught by parents or friends the lesson of his Messiahship, whose faith is at this moment as fresh, strong, and as devoted as that of the martyr of the olden time.

To illustrate their faith and the terrible infatuation with which they were beset, the following incident is presented: It was communicated to us by a gentleman who was a personal witness of what is related, and who has aided us much in obtaining facts connected with the delusion.

In the summer of 1850, a large man, about thirty-five years of age, stopped for dinner at the hotel of Mr. Robert Mills, in Barnesville, Ohio. He was dressed in an uncolored homespun suit, cut after the plain style of the old Methodists, and wore his hair and beard long and disheveled. He had a fine horse, saddle and bridle, and on the valise pad was strapped a small, flat box. Having dismounted, he carefully unstrapped the box and carried it under his arms into the setting-room of the hotel. When invited to dinner, he took the box with him and placed it on the floor by the side of his chair. After dinner he brought the box into the bar room and instantly inquired if any one in the room wished to see a rattlesnake : if so, he would show one for a "dime a-peice." Quite a crowd had, by this time assembled to see the queer-acting stranger. A purse was soon made up. The stranger opened the box and a large rattlesnake, having eighteen rattles, emerged from it, and coiled itself on the floor. It was lively and seemed rejoiced to see its master, shook its rattles, threw open its mouth and shot out its tounge. The snake was fangless. One of the spectators seeing this, inquired the cause. The man replied :

"When I caught it, I took it up and knocked out its teeth with my Jacknife."

"Were you not afraid to take hold of it ?" was asked.

"No : for had it bit me, it would have done me no harm. I shall never die I shall live three hundred and fifty years, precisely, from this year, and shall then be transferred into the New Jerusalem without seeing death."

He then proceeded for over an hour to expatiate upon the claims of Dylks, saying that he often saw Dylks in the spirit—had frequent conversations with him—and had been informed by him, that before the end of the present century, he should descend to earth and establish a kingdom of universal righteousness.

This stranger gave his name as Moses Hartley, and resided in the mountains of what is now West Virginia. He had been on a visit to the "Temple." "The only place" as he said, "where true religion had ever been produced."